D0791640

Essential Skills Book 20

Twenty-five Passages
with Questions for
Developing the Six
Essential Categories
of Comprehension

Walter Pauk, Ph.D.
Director, Reading-
Study Center
Cornell University

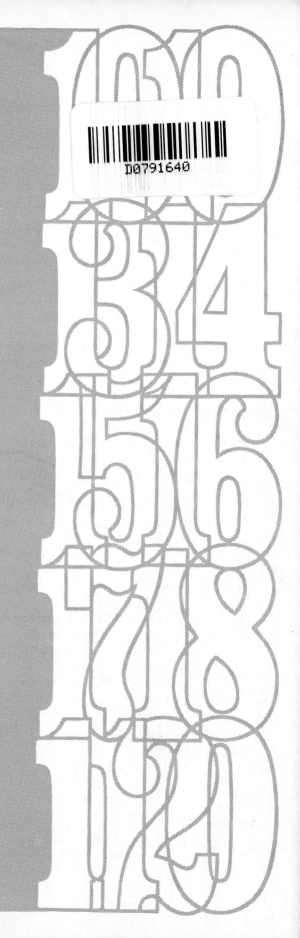

Jamestown Publishers

PREFACE

Why do boys shoot baskets over and over again and girls skate and reskate the same routine? These beginners know that practice makes perfect. Not only do beginners know this, but pros do too. For what other reason do they work at baseball and football week after week before the opening dates?

The pros know the value of practice, but they also know the value of something else. They know that practice without *instruction* and *guidance* does not automatically lead to improvement. That's why they have the best coaches that money can buy.

And so it is with developing the skills of reading. There must be the right kind of practicing and the right kind of coaching.

First, a word about practice. In this book the right kind of practice is provided by 25 articles, highly interesting and carefully selected. Here is material enough on which to grow and keep growing.

Now about coaching! Good coaching takes the form of instruction and guidance. In this book the instruction is straightforward and uncomplicated. It puts you directly on the right track, and better still, you are kept on the right track by two unusual systems of guidance. The first system is the uniquely-designed, six-way-question format which makes sure that every ounce of practice is directed toward improvement. Nothing is wasted!

The second system of guidance is the Diagnostic Chart. This chart is no ordinary gimmick. In truth, it provides the most dignified form of diagnosis and guidance yet devised. It provides instantaneous and continuous diagnosis and gentle but certain self-guidance. It yields information directly to the student. There is no middleman. No one needs to needle him. This form of self-guidance leads to the goal of all education: the goal of self-learning.

Now, I want to make some acknowledgements, especially to the students who were the guinea pigs. Afterwards I told them so, but they said, "We didn't mind even then. And now that it is over, we're all the happier because we know how much we've learned." But what the students did not know was how much I learned from them. For this I thank them all, class after class.

I direct especial thanks to Linda Browning for handling the almost countless number of selections, writing and refining the questions and making sure that the series kept moving: all, a most demanding task.

Finally, I am most grateful to authors, editors and publishers who have generously given permission to quote and reprint in this book from works written and published by them. The books quoted in the text and used as sources of reading extracts are listed in the back of the booklet. — W.P.

Essential Skills Series
ESS-20, Book 20, Grade 12B, ISBN 0-89061-119-X

CONTENTS

ORGANIZATION OF THE BOOKLETS

Selection Criteria. Twenty-five of the very best articles obtainable were selected for each booklet. Each article had to meet, at least, the following criteria: *high interest level, appropriate readability level,* and *factual accuracy of contents.*

High interest was assured by choosing passages from popular magazines that appeal to a wide range of readers. The readability level of each passage was determined by the use of the Dale-Chall readability formula, thus enabling the arrangement of passages on a single grade level within each booklet. The factual accuracy of the passages is high because they were written by professional writers whose works are recognized and respected.

The Questions. At the end of each passage there are six questions to answer. The six questions will always be within the framework of the following six categories: subject matter; main ideas; supporting details; conclusions; clarifying devices; and vocabulary in context. By repeated practice with questions within these six essential categories, students will develop an active, searching attitude when reading other expository prose. These questions will help them become aware of what they are reading at the time of the actual perception of the words and phrases, thus building high comprehension.

The Diagnostic Chart. Fast and sure improvement in reading comprehension can be made by using the Diagnostic Chart to identify relative strengths and weaknesses. The Diagnostic Chart is a very efficient instrument. Here is how it works.

The questions for every passage are always in the same order. For example, the question designed to teach the skill of recognizing the *main idea* is always in the number two position, and the skill of drawing *conclusions* is always in the number four position, and so on.

The Diagnostic Chart functions automatically when the letters of answers are placed in the proper spaces. Even after completing one passage, the chart will reveal the types of questions answered correctly, as well as the types answered incorrectly. But more important for the long run is that the chart will identify the types of questions that are missed consistently. Once a weakness (in drawing conclusions, for example) is ascertained, the following procedure is recommended: First, the student should reread the question; then, with the correct answer in mind, he should reread the entire passage trying to perceive how the author actually did lead to or imply the correct conclusion. Second, on succeeding passages, he should put forth extra effort to answer correctly the questions pertaining to drawing conclusions. Third, if the difficulty continues, he should arrange a conference with his teacher.

TEACHING THE SIX ESSENTIAL SKILLS

What reading skills does a person have to know to gain meaning from factual prose? To gain meaning, most people would have to know, at least, six essential skills. They would have to know how to concentrate to glean the subject matter, to grasp main ideas, to relate supporting details to main ideas and sub-ideas, to draw conclusions, to recognize clarifying devices, and to unlock the meaning of words. Let's take a closer look at these skills.

Concentration/Subject Matter

There is no problem that I hear more frequently than, "I can't concentrate!" Fortunately, there's a sure, fast cure. There is no better magic for gaining concentration while reading than this one: After reading the first few lines of a selection, softly ask yourself this question, "What is this article about?" In other words, "What's the general subject matter?"

If you don't ask this question, here's what will generally happen: Your eyes will move across the lines of print while your mind is still entertaining the lingering thoughts of a previous conversation or daydream.

If you ask the question, however, you will almost always arrive at an answer, thus capturing concentration. Let's see whether or not this technique works. Here are the first lines of an article:

> Wood ducks are the most beautiful ducks in America. Once they
> were rare. Now — if you have sharp eyes and can keep quiet — you
> might see them in almost any woodland, along streams and ponds.

Obviously, you can say with a great degree of assurance that the author is going to talk about the wood duck. Now that your mind is on the trail, the chances are great it will follow the author's ideas paragraph after paragraph, thereby *concentrating* on the development of the subject matter.

Let's try the technique again. Here are a few lines from another article:

> Of all the little animals in the world, the Columbian ground squirrel
> is one of the liveliest and friendliest. He is nicknamed "picket pin"
> because he sits as stiff and straight as a stake on the ground.

Again, you probably experienced no trouble at all zeroing in on the subject matter: the Columbian ground squirrel.

The Main Idea

Once the general subject matter has been quickly ascertained, it is easier for the mind to grapple with the next question: What is the author's main idea? What point is he trying to get across?

With such questions in mind, it is surprising how often an answer pops up. When no questions are asked, it seems that everything is on the same level — nothing stands out.

Let us peruse another short excerpt, this time for the main idea.

> Wood ducks never nest on the ground as most ducks do, but in a
> big hole in a tree. Trees with big holes in them are hard to find.

Since you don't have the full article to read, may I make this comment: The main point that the author is making is that with the scarcity of old, dead trees with holes in them, we will have fewer and fewer wood ducks.

Thus, we see that by asking questions, reading becomes a two-way street. When we talk with the author, the article seems to come to life. Reading then becomes an exciting and enjoyable experience.

Supporting Details

Are we interested in details? Of course we are! In longer articles, main ideas and sub-ideas are the bones, the skeleton of the articles. The details are the flesh which gives articles completeness, fullness and life.

Details are used almost entirely to support the main idea and sub-ideas. Consequently, the term *supporting details* is appropriate. These supporting details come in various forms, but the most common forms are: examples, definitions, comparisons and contrasts, repetitions and descriptions.

The author of "The Wood Duck" has supplied us with enough information so that we know the article is about wood ducks. Next, he made sure that we understood the point that without "trees with big holes in them" the wood duck will not nest; thus, there would be fewer wood ducks.

Having gotten us interested in this unique problem, he then supplied details on how we could provide "trees with big holes in them." He *described* how we could build a wood duck nesting box. Here's the excerpt:

> Why don't you and your parents put up wood duck nesting boxes
> right now? It would be about 2 feet high and 10 inches square. Make
> the entry hole about four inches in diameter. Use rough lumber on the
> inside so the ducklings can climb up the sides to the hole. Put wood
> shavings in the bottom in which the duck will lay her eggs. To keep her
> eggs warm, she covers them with her own feathers. If you don't have a
> tree near the water, you'll need a post. Place the box 10 to 30 feet high.

You can see in the above example how important details are in telling a story. Details enable the reader to visualize what's going on, how to do something, how to take action, and so forth.

In any article of length, there will be some or many sub-ideas. It is important to be sufficiently wary so as not to mistake a sub-idea for a main idea. One way to distinguish between the two is as follows: The main idea pertains to the entire article, whereas the sub-idea pertains only to a portion of it. Notice that in the following example the sub-idea is about the food which wood ducks eat. The entire article is *not* about food, so it is *not* the main idea. In most cases you will see that a sub-idea takes the space of one paragraph.

The main purpose for including the following excerpts is to show how the author clusters and organizes his supporting details around the relatively minor sub-ideas which are stated in topic sentences. In other words, a sub-idea is the nucleus which holds a body of details together.

> Wood ducks like to eat acorns and all kinds of nuts. Their stomachs (or gizzards) have such powerful muscles that they can break the hardest nuts, some that you could barely crack with a hammer! Wood ducks like berries, duckweed and insects. But best of all they like to eat spiders — that's ice cream to them.

The author, after adding to the article a brief but detailed description of some food which wood ducks eat, continues on to describe how the newly hatched ducklings get down to the ground from some dizzy heights. Here are more details clustered around another sub-idea.

> Sometimes they nest in holes up in trees that are twice as high as a flagpole. Just think, the baby ducklings must jump to the ground the day they hatch. Usually they don't get hurt, though, because they're light, like little puffs of cotton. The mother stands at the foot of the tree and calls and calls. Like little paratroopers, the ducklings peek out of the hole, then jump quickly, one right after the other, to join their mother, who must hurry them to the pond where they're safe.

Thus, one of the main functions of *supporting details* is to give some dimension to an article. Otherwise, it would be a rather uninteresting, skimpy statement of one main idea together with its bare-boned sub-ideas. The examples, descriptions, explanations, etc., are what give life to the article.

Conclusions

As a reader moves through an article, understanding the main idea, the sub-ideas and their supporting details, it is only natural for him to anticipate a conclusion to the author's story. Such anticipation is part of the sport of reading. Frequently, though, the author provides the reader with a conclusion. In such an event, the joy of reading lies in the fact that the reader was able to anticipate accurately the conclusion. In the event that a conclusion is not stated, the perceptive reader will be able to seize the implied conclusion.

From the excerpts just read about the wood duck, the conclusion is in the form of having the reader visualize the pleasure of having a wood duck to observe. The concluding sentence is this:

> If you're lucky, though, and if your (duck) house is in place before the ice melts, you will have a wood duck family in the summer.

In another selection entitled "From Pond to Prairie," the author has this as his conclusion:

> Finally, there is no longer much open water. The pond has disappeared. Depending on the kinds of plants that have filled it, the pond

may be called a bog or a marsh. As changes continue for many more
years, the bog may become a forest.

The reader who reads with speed and comprehension is the reader who, like
a detective, follows the maze of ideas and details and descriptions, but who
is always thinking, "Where is the author leading me? What's his final point?
What's his conclusion?" And, of course, like a detective, the reader must
continually anticipate a conclusion, always correcting or reinforcing his
anticipations as he takes in more and more of the story or selection.

Clarifying Devices

Just as the name implies, the author uses everything that he can possibly
think of to make his points clear and interesting. In a sense, the much-
mentioned *topic sentence* may be thought of as a clarifying device. By
placing it at the very beginning of a passage, the author provides the reader
with an immediate point of focus, as well as a definite statement from which
the reader can anticipate what is to come.

But usually, by clarifying devices, we mean the author's use of literary
devices, such as transitional words and phrases which keep the ideas, sub-
ideas and details in proper relationship.

To make ideas as well as details clear and interesting in themselves,
authors frequently use additional literary devices such as the *metaphor*,
an example of which follows: But best of all they like to eat spiders — *that's
ice cream to them.*

Another literary device which authors frequently use is the *simile: Like
little paratroopers,* the ducklings peek out of the hole, then jump quickly,
one right after the other. The simile about the paratroopers provides the
reader with familiar material which helps him to visualize the scene more
graphically and vividly.

In addition to transitional words and phrases, metaphors and similes,
there are many other types of *clarifying devices*. Another cluster of clarifying devices are the organizational patterns. One such pattern is the chrono-
logical pattern in which the events unfold in the order of time; that is, one
thing happens first, and then another, and another, and so forth.

The time pattern may give structure and control to an incident that takes
place in a span of five minutes or to an historical era which may span
hundreds of years. Or, used in another way, the time pattern may be the
vehicle used to sequence the activities of an animal from birth to death or
even to delineate the sequence of events in a transition.

By knowing some of these clarifying devices, you will be able to recognize
them in the selections that you read, and, by recognizing them, you will
be able to read with greater comprehension and with greater speed.

Vocabulary in Context

Of course, if a reader doesn't understand some of the words and terms in
a selection, he runs the risk of misconstruing the author's ideas. It should be

obvious that a reader should pause to look up in a dictionary the words and terms that he does not know.

However, what is not so obvious is that many readers who may understand the general meaning of a word don't stop to look up such a word to ascertain its *precise* meaning.

When such a reader imposes upon a generally understood word his rather general understanding, he may end up with a blurred picture of the idea. Whereas, when he imposes a precise and full meaning upon a word, his chances of emerging with a precise and full picture of the author's idea are immensely enhanced.

For example, in the following excerpt are two common words which most people feel they already know. Consequently, they don't see any reason for any dictionary work. Nevertheless, few people know them with the precision the words deserve.

> **Depending on the kinds of plants that have filled it, the pond may be called a *bog* or a *marsh*.**

Do you know the difference between a bog and a marsh? Is there a difference? If so, what is it? Would your mental picture be different if you knew?

Looking up words which you think you already know might be far more rewarding than simply seeking to add more totally unknown words to your vocabulary. In other words, strive for a smaller but *precise* vocabulary, rather than for a broader but slightly blurred vocabulary.

Looking up words you feel you already know will probably take more discipline than looking up unknown words. Here are some words that are likely to be unknown; so, turning to the dictionary is almost a reflex action:

> **Nothing could appear more *benign* than a field aglow with daisies, goldenrod and Queen Anne's lace.**

> ***Sphinxlike*, it crouches among the flowers until the desired insect wanders within reach.**

Thus, the dictionary is the stock market where we can exchange fuzzy meanings and soft meanings for precise meanings and where we can acquire new meanings for unknown words and all this at no cost other than a flip of the finger.

GETTING THE MOST OUT OF THIS BOOKLET

The steps given below for you to follow could be called "tricks of the trade." Your teachers might call them "rules for learning." It doesn't matter what they are called. What does matter is that they work.

Think About the Title

A good reader we know told us about a "trick" he uses every time he reads. He said, "The first thing I do is read the title. Then I spend a few moments thinking about it."

Writers spend a lot of time thinking up good titles. They try to pack as much meaning as possible into them. It makes sense, then, for the reader to spend a few seconds trying to get the full meaning out. These few moments of thought give the reader a head start on the story.

Thinking about the title can help you in another way, too. It starts you off concentrating on the story before you actually begin reading it. Why does this happen? Thinking about the title fills your head so full of thoughts about the story that there's no room for anything else to get in to break concentration.

If you have trouble concentrating when you read, try this step. It works!

The Dot System

Here is a step that will speed up your reading and build comprehension at the same time.

After spending a few moments with the title, read *quickly* through the passage. Then, without looking back, answer the six questions, using a dot. For each question, place a dot in the box beside the answer of your choice. The dots will be your "unofficial" answers.

The dot system helps by making you work a little harder on your first, *fast* reading. The effort you make to grasp and retain ideas makes you a better reader.

The Check-Mark System

After you have answered all of the questions with a dot, read the story again, *carefully*. This time, make your final answers to the questions using a check mark (✓). For each question, place a check mark in the box next to the answer of your choice. The answers with the check marks are the ones that will count toward your score.

The Diagnostic Chart

Now, transfer your final answers to the diagnostic chart on page 64. Use the column of boxes under number 1 for the answers to the first passage; use the column of boxes under number 2 for the answers to the second story, and so on.

Write the letter of your answer in the *upper* portion of each block.

Correct your answers using the answer key on page 63. When scoring your answers, do *not* use an *x* for *incorrect* or a *c* for *correct*. Instead, follow this method. If your answer is correct, make no mark in the answer block; leave it alone. If your answer is *incorrect*, write the letter of the correct answer in the *lower* portion of the block, underneath your wrong answer.

Properly used, then, the answer column for each story will show not only your incorrect answers, but also what the correct answers should be. This sets the stage for the next step.

Taking Corrective Action

Your incorrect answers give you a real opportunity for self-learning. Take this opportunity to study your wrong answers. Go back to the original question and read the correct answer several times. With the correct answer in mind, go back to the story itself. Read to see why the approved answer is best. Try to see where you made your mistake. Try to see why you chose a wrong answer.

Graphing Your Progress

Underneath the diagnostic chart on page 64 is a progress graph for you to use. For each story, put an *x* where the lines cross to show your score. Join the *x*'s as you go; plot a line showing your progress.

The Steps in a Nutshell

Here's a quick review of the steps you have just read:

1. Think About the Title. Get from the title all the meaning the writer put into it.

2. The Dot System. After your first, fast reading, answer the six questions using a dot. The dots are your unofficial answers.

3. The Check-Mark System. Read the passage again, carefully this time. Put a check mark (✓) in the box beside your final answer.

4. The Diagnostic Chart. Record your final answers in the upper blocks on the chart on page 64. Use the column of blocks under the number of the passage you have just read.

5. The Answer Key. Using the key on page 63, correct your answers. Leave correct answers alone. Write the approved answers in the boxes underneath your incorrect ones.

6. Taking Correct Action. Study all of your wrong answers. Read the story again. Try to see why and where you were wrong.

7. Graphing Your Progress. Plot your scores on the graph on page 64. Join the *x*'s to show your line of progress.

1. SHARK ATTACK!

Toward the end of the last century, a New York financier, Herman Oelrichs, heir to a shipping fortune, offered $500 to anyone who could prove that a shark had attacked a man north of Cape Hatteras, North Carolina. Until he died in 1906, the reward was never claimed — tacit evidence that sharks do not attack in northern waters, or so it seemed. In April, 1916, three prominent New York scientists, in an article on sharks in the "Brooklyn Museum Quarterly," disparaged the very idea of a shark attack on a man and said: ". . . there is practically no danger of any attack from a shark about our coasts."

Then, three months later, on the first day of July, 1916, a crowd of holiday bathers saw a shark attack and kill a young man at Beach Haven, New Jersey, about 90 miles from New York City. Within a week, a shark killed another man at Spring Lake, New Jersey, less than 50 miles from New York. A few days later, in Matawan Creek, a shark killed a boy, a man and seriously injured another boy. Matawan Creek is about 30 miles from New York. Soon after, a 7-foot, great white shark was caught in Sandy Hook Bay at the mouth of New York Harbor, and in its belly were 15 pounds of flesh. One of the scientists, who had so recently dismissed the danger of shark attack, identified the flesh as human.

Thus, dramatically, the shark changed its image. No longer a harmless wild creature, it became the villain who preempted the headlines as it emptied the beaches. World War I was inflaming Europe. A polio epidemic was raging in New York, but the shark had all the headlines in the metropolitan papers. Vacationers deserted the beach resorts despite the pleadings of businessmen who assured them that there were no more sharks than there ever were. This was scant comfort to those so rudely and so recently awakened to the potential danger from sharks. The resorts lost an estimated $1 million in the summer of 1916.

1. This passage is primarily about
   - □ a. different kinds of sharks.
   - □ b. sharks and humans.
   - □ c. the shark family.
   - □ d. sizes of sharks.

2. Sharks
   - □ a. are harmless creatures.
   - □ b. never attack swimmers.
   - □ c. make good parents.
   - □ d. can be dangerous.

3. The shark in this article is a
   - □ a. hammerhead shark.
   - □ b. tiger shark.
   - □ c. great white shark.
   - □ d. whale shark.

4. We can guess that sharks
   - □ a. are able to swim in shallow water.
   - □ b. never venture too close to shore.
   - □ c. travel in schools.
   - □ d. mate for life.

5. The vacationers in this article deserted the beaches because
   - □ a. they were afraid.
   - □ b. the weather was foul.
   - □ c. the water became polluted.
   - □ d. the sun became too hot.

6. A villain is someone who is
   - □ a. calm.
   - □ b. good-natured.
   - □ c. helpful.
   - □ d. evil.

CATEGORIES OF COMPREHENSION QUESTIONS

No. 1: Subject Matter	No. 3: Supporting Details	No. 5: Clarifying Devices
No. 2: Main Idea	No. 4: Conclusion	No. 6: Vocabulary in Context

2. WHAT IS A SHARK?

Sharks are like bony fish in that they are fish-shaped, breathe through gills and live in water, but there the similarity ends. They have five to seven gill openings instead of one on each side of the head, their skin is not covered with orthodox fish scales but with minute teeth (denticles) that have one or more ridges with sharp projections which make the skin alone a formidable weapon. One man, whose legs were lashed by a shark's tail, spent two weeks in a hospital recovering from the injury. Sharkskin is often used for sandpaper under the name "shagreen." Sharks' skeletons are formed entirely of cartilage. This complete lack of bone is a decided advantage when sharkmeat is on the menu. The vertebral column of sharks extends into the upper lobe of the tail and is responsible for that characteristic "shark" look. The absence of a swim bladder prohibits sharks from "hovering" in the water as bony fish do. They must either swim or sink.

Sharks' teeth are usually large, sharp and attached in rows to the skin of their jaws. Special ligaments and muscles enable sharks both to erect their teeth and to project their jaws. As many as five rows of teeth may be ready for use, and, when one tooth is lost, it is replaced by another rolling out from a seemingly endless supply which develops constantly on the inner margin of the jaws.

The keen sense organs of sharks account in large measure for their success as predators. Smell is highly developed and most, if not all, of the forebrain is devoted to the olfactory sense. The two nostrils are situated on the underside of the head and do not connect with the mouth. Sea water flows continuously through incurrent and excurrent nostril openings over the sense cells of each olfactory sac. The eyes of sharks are well adapted for perceiving an object, especially a moving one, in either bright or dim light.

Mechanical disturbances in the water are detected by hundreds of tiny pressure receptors called "pit organs" located between the denticles on extensive portions of the body. A well-developed system of fluid-filled sensory canals also plays an important role in detecting water-borne vibrations.

1. This article centers mostly on a shark's
   ☐ a. diet.
   ☐ b. nature.
   ☐ c. appearance.
   ☐ d. natural habitat.

2. The writer's main idea is
   ☐ a. to compare two species of sharks.
   ☐ b. to explain the shark's violent nature.
   ☐ c. to show how sharks migrate.
   ☐ d. to inform us about sharks in general.

3. Instead of scales, sharks have minute teeth called
   ☐ a. denticles.
   ☐ b. dentifrice.
   ☐ c. dentine.
   ☐ d. dentition.

4. A swim bladder
   ☐ a. helps a fish digest bony material.
   ☐ b. helps a fish breathe.
   ☐ c. is used in reproduction.
   ☐ d. keeps a fish from sinking.

5. Sharkskin can be described as
   ☐ a. smooth.
   ☐ b. rough.
   ☐ c. sticky.
   ☐ d. soft.

6. Olfactory has to do with the sense of
   ☐ a. seeing.
   ☐ b. hearing.
   ☐ c. smelling.
   ☐ d. touching.

CATEGORIES OF COMPREHENSION QUESTIONS

| No. 1: Subject Matter | No. 3: Supporting Details | No. 5: Clarifying Devices |
| No. 2: Main Idea | No. 4: Conclusion | No. 6: Vocabulary in Context |

3. FISH 'N CHIPS ANYONE?

The spiny dogfish is a small (2 feet to 4 feet) slender shark, with a quill-like spine in front of each of its two dorsal fins. It is the most abundant shark in the western North Atlantic and the only shark which can rival in population the commercial fishes. They are slow swimmers, readily take a hook and offer little resistance to being caught. Some live to be thirty years old.

The spiny dogfish occurs in temperate and subarctic latitudes on both sides of the Atlantic and Pacific oceans. They have a well-defined seasonal migration, north in spring and south in fall. In addition, they move to deep water by day and shallow water at night.

They are capable of swimming great distances in a short time, up to 7.6 miles in one day or 1,000 miles in 132 days. One tagged dogfish traveled 4,700 miles.

Male dogfish are eleven years old before they mature sexually, and the female, incredibly, is not sexually mature until she is eighteen to twenty-one years old. Mating takes place in February or March far out at sea. The large-yolked eggs develop within the mother's body, and after nearly two years four to ten young are born. This twenty-two-month pregnancy is the longest of any vertebrate, longer even than the elephant's.

Dogfish in general are opportunistic feeders. They eat fish and invertebrates of any species available. In contrast, they are the prey of a very limited number of fish and marine animals. Perhaps their spines and tough hides make them unpalatable.

The spiny dogfish is the most destructive fish in the sea. Schools of dogfish descend like swarms of locusts on a fishing ground, devour the fish and destroy the nets. They will eat indiscriminately either the bait or the hooked fish. When the food supply is exhausted, they move on to greener pastures. They are the bane of the fisherman's existence since there is no food market for the dogfish on the eastern seaboard. Fresh-cooked dogfish is very palatable, tastes like haddock and is used extensively in Europe as a food fish. In London, it is often the fish used in "fish 'n chips."

1. The spiny dogfish is a kind of
   ☐ a. sunfish.
   ☑ b. shark.
   ☐ c. whale.
   ☐ d. crab.

2. The main idea of this selection is
   ☐ a. to acquaint the reader with spiny dogfish.
   ☐ b. to show the mating habits of the dogfish.
   ☐ c. to discuss the nature of the spiny dogfish.
   ☐ d. to compare the dogfish to bony fish.

3. The female dogfish carries the unborn in her body
   ☐ a. ten months.
   ☐ b. twelve months.
   ☐ c. eighteen months.
   ☑ d. twenty-two months.

4. This article leads us to believe that the spiny dogfish
   ☐ a. can be raised in captivity.
   ☐ b. will attack a human.
   ☑ c. is not usually found in tropical waters.
   ☐ d. feeds mostly on plankton.

5. Fresh cooked dogfish is
   ☐ a. tasty.
   ☐ b. salty.
   ☐ c. unedible.
   ☐ d. tough.

6. Devour means
   ☐ a. to chase.
   ☐ b. to hunt.
   ☐ c. to frighten.
   ☑ d. to eat greedily.

CATEGORIES OF COMPREHENSION QUESTIONS

No. 1: Subject Matter	No. 3: Supporting Details	No. 5: Clarifying Devices
No. 2: Main Idea	No. 4: Conclusion	No. 6: Vocabulary in Context

4. GREAT BLUES AHOY!

The great blue shark is probably the most beautiful and certainly the most abundant of the large oceanic sharks. It is long (up to 12 feet) and slender with narrow, graceful pectoral fins. It has a deep indigo blue back, bright blue sides and a white belly. It occurs in all the tropic, subtropic and temperate seas of the world. Frequently, it basks at the surface in temperate climates, while in the tropics it inhabits the deeper, cooler waters. Primarily a deep sea species, it often approaches shore in pursuit of food.

Great blues gather like flies when a whale is harpooned and feast voraciously, frequently exciting themselves into a "feeding frenzy" when they will eat anything in sight, even each other. Naturally, they are detested by whalemen. Their usual food, however, is the small life of the seas, fish and invertebrates, especially squid, occasionally a bird.

There is no doubt at all that this shark is potentially dangerous to man. It has all the necessary apparatus — razor-sharp teeth, swift, powerful body and a voracious appetite. However, there are no authentic records of its ever having attacked anyone.

The great blue shark gives birth to between twenty-eight and fifty-four young, a large litter for a shark. Birth takes place in the eastern Atlantic. Most of the blues caught off Cornwall, England, are females who have come to "nursery grounds" to give birth to their young. Those caught in the vicinity of New York and in the western Atlantic are generally males. Such segregation of the sexes is essential to their survival because of their cannibalistic tendencies. Most female sharks of every species fast when they are in the nursery grounds, another factor imperative for the survival of the young. There is no maternal care among sharks.

The great blues are of little economic importance except to the whaling industry and to the game fishing industry. They readily take a bait, violently resist capture and are officially listed as a game fish.

1. The great blues are mostly
   ☐ a. shallow water dwellers.
   ☐ b. tidal pool inhabitants.
   ☐ c. salt marsh animals.
   ☐ d. deep sea creatures.

2. Great blues are the
   ☐ a. smallest of all fish.
   ☐ b. largest shark known to man.
   ☐ c. most numerous of ocean sharks.
   ☐ d. rarest of all sharks.

3. A litter for great blues ranges between
   ☐ a. two and eight.
   ☐ b. ten and twenty-two.
   ☐ c. twenty and twenty-five.
   ☐ d. twenty-eight and fifty-four.

4. Which of the following is most likely true?
   ☐ a. Great blues are on their own from birth.
   ☐ b. There is a great demand for great blues for aquariums.
   ☐ c. It is difficult to find a great blue.
   ☐ d. Great blues feed only on plant life.

5. A "feeding frenzy" would look
   ☐ a. peaceful.
   ☐ b. organized.
   ☐ c. violent.
   ☐ d. inviting.

6. These creatures are sometimes cannibalistic. This means they may
   ☐ a. hunt together.
   ☐ b. eat each other.
   ☐ c. share their food equally.
   ☐ d. refuse to eat.

CATEGORIES OF COMPREHENSION QUESTIONS

| No. 1: Subject Matter | No. 3: Supporting Details | No. 5: Clarifying Devices |
| No. 2: Main Idea | No. 4: Conclusion | No. 6: Vocabulary in Context |

5. MAN-EATER ON THE PROWL

Probably the most famous, or infamous, of all sharks is the great white shark, commonly called the man-eater. It is readily recognized by its massive, deep-bellied build. It is dark above, light gray or white below. Its first dorsal fin is triangular and five or six times the size of the second dorsal. The tail is half-moon shaped and nearly symmetrical.

The great white shark swims constantly at about 10 knots per hour, which is equal to 11-1/2 miles per hour. Its balance is remarkable, due perhaps to the two horizontal keels on each side of the tail and to the long pectoral fins. The skin of the great white, surprisingly, is not very tough to the touch because the tiny dermal denticles have three almost flat ridges.

The teeth are triangular, large (up to 2 inches high), serrated and razor-sharp. Placed in rows in the large powerful jaws, they are a formidable armament and an efficient instrument for the seizure and cutting of prey.

The great white shark feeds on all the large, warm-blooded and cold-blooded animals of the sea, such as seals, sea turtles, fish, sharks and a variety of smaller animals like squid and chimaeroids. It is also a scavenger; parts of horses, pigs and dogs have been found in its belly. It slices the tough shell of the sea turtle like butter, but in its greed it often swallows prey whole.

Always hungry and utterly unafraid, this is the shark most dangerous to man. It is guilty of more attacks on men and boats than any other shark. Frequently, with no provocation, it slams into a boat and leaves a tooth embedded in the fractured hull, as reliable as a calling card, for positive identification of the culprit.

1. The man-eater is the
   ☐ a. sand shark.
   ☐ b. great white shark.
   ☐ c. leopard shark.
   ☐ d. black-tipped shark.

2. According to this article, the man-eater is
   ☐ a. similar to the whale in several respects.
   ☐ b. probably easy to capture.
   ☐ c. the smallest of sharks.
   ☐ d. perhaps the most famous of all sharks.

3. The great white shark is
   ☐ a. the most dangerous of all sharks.
   ☐ b. not as dangerous as the great blue shark.
   ☐ c. very helpful to man.
   ☐ d. the largest of all sharks.

4. Evidently, this man-eater
   ☐ a. can be tamed.
   ☐ b. is becoming extinct.
   ☐ c. is actually gentle and calm.
   ☐ d. is very aggressive.

5. A "calling card" is a
   ☐ a. chartered fishing trip.
   ☐ b. long period of time.
   ☐ c. trademark for identification.
   ☐ d. half-moon shape.

6. Another word for embedded is
   ☐ a. on top of.
   ☐ b. attached.
   ☐ c. buried.
   ☐ d. encrusted.

CATEGORIES OF COMPREHENSION QUESTIONS

No. 1: Subject Matter	No. 3: Supporting Details	No. 5: Clarifying Devices
No. 2: Main Idea	No. 4: Conclusion	No. 6: Vocabulary in Context

6. TIGERS OF THE SEA

The tiger shark is probably the most common large shark in the tropics. In the summer, it enters temperate waters. It may range far out to sea but is frequently found in shallow waters. Normally a slow swimmer, it is swift in chase.

The tiger shark is quite large (up to 18 feet), gray or grayish brown above, lighter below. The younger ones have darker brown, irregular, vertical bars on the sides which account for the name "tiger."

The serrated teeth of the tiger shark are easily recognized. They are triangular with the tip directed outward. They are large (up to 1 inch high) at the front of the jaws, smaller at the corners.

Hinges at the center of the upper and lower jaw and an elastic articulation at the sides permit the tiger shark to open its mouth unusually wide. Using the large teeth like a saw, it is capable of biting large chunks of tough food, the shell of a turtle, for instance. By efficiently chopping its food into pieces, one tiger shark 12 feet long ate another tiger shark 10 feet long.

This is the shark whose insatiable appetite has accounted for its eating all sorts of inedible and incredible items such as a keg of nails, a roll of roofing paper, old shoes and a bottle of fine Madeira wine! It often is accused of attacking man in Australia and ample evidence exists to implicate it as the culprit in several attacks on humans along the southwestern Atlantic coast of the United States. Their usual food is fish, invertebrates, turtles, birds, sea snakes and sharks. They also are scavengers of the oceans and are useful refuse collectors.

The tiger shark hide tans into a high grade leather, the liver yields a large quantity of oil and the teeth are a favorite of the curio and jewelry trade. On the negative side, the tiger shark does extensive and costly damage to the nets and catch of fishermen. Outweighing all its other demerits is the dread it generates when sighted near a bathing beach, and the revulsion and horror it produces by its occasional attacks on man.

1. Select the best title.
   - ☐ a. The Shy Tiger Shark
   - ☐ b. Tiger Sharks Make Good Parents
   - ☐ c. Sandbar Fish
   - ☐ d. Characteristics of the Tiger Shark

2. The writer's main idea is
   - ☐ a. to tell us many facts about the tiger shark.
   - ☐ b. to show us how tiger sharks migrate.
   - ☐ c. to describe the tiger shark and its family.
   - ☐ d. to discuss the near extinction of the tiger shark.

3. Tiger sharks are the most common large shark of
   - ☐ a. tropical waters.
   - ☐ b. arctic waters.
   - ☐ c. the Mediterranean Sea.
   - ☐ d. the North Sea.

4. Tiger sharks are sometimes
   - ☐ a. poisonous.
   - ☐ b. cannabalistic.
   - ☐ c. caught sunbathing.
   - ☐ d. shy and docile.

5. This shark gets its name from its tigerlike
   - ☐ a. eyes.
   - ☐ b. jaws.
   - ☐ c. appearance.
   - ☐ d. nature.

6. Serrated teeth are
   - ☐ a. weak.
   - ☐ b. notched.
   - ☐ c. removable.
   - ☐ d. smooth.

CATEGORIES OF COMPREHENSION QUESTIONS

No. 1: Subject Matter	No. 3: Supporting Details	No. 5: Clarifying Devices
No. 2: Main Idea	No. 4: Conclusion	No. 6: Vocabulary in Context

7. DOMINENT DENIZEN OF THE DEEP!

In the United States, the shark was officially recognized as a major menace during World War II when servicemen were reluctant to fly or sail over shark-infested waters. Tales, unfortunately true, of sharks feasting on the victims of military disasters caused such low morale that in 1942 the United States Navy instituted a crash program in a hurried search for a defense against sharks. The result was Shark Chaser, a fair but not always foolproof repellent.

In subsequent years, scientists have searched for more effective repellents with qualified success. Innumerable chemical, mechanical and electrical devices have been tested. Many succeeded in repelling one or more species of shark in a controlled situation. None has consistently repelled all species of sharks when widely tested, and none has deterred sharks when they are in a feeding frenzy. There is a wide variation of response among different species and even among individuals of the same species. For instance, one tiger shark refused to swim across a bubble curtain; eleven other tiger sharks had no such inhibitions.

The activities of our present fishing industry favor the shark. Not only are sharks not fished for intensively, which in essence gives them a "protected" status, but they are even nurtured by being fed the discarded fish and entrails jettisoned into the sea after the fishermen sort and clean their catch.

Where shark fisheries operate, the number of sharks decrease markedly. In Australia and South Africa, meshing of bathing beaches has greatly reduced the number of shark attacks. Meshing is actually a fishing operation. Gill nets are placed parallel to the beach, off shore, and sharks are caught by their gills as they swim through them. No bather has been attacked while swimming at a meshed beach.

Undoubtedly, the most effective control of sharks will be the increased use of them for food, fishmeal, fertilizer, leather, oil, glue, curios, jewelry and laboratory animals. As populations increase and as our oceans become increasingly the habitat of men, it is imperative that sharks relinquish their position of dominance in the sea. Instead of the bane of man, let them become the benefactors of man.

24

1. Choose the best title.
   ☐ a. Uses of Sharkskin
   ☐ b. Sand Sharks Don't Bite
   ☐ c. How To Avoid Attack
   ☐ d. Shark Control

2. The shark is considered
   ☐ a. the best game fish alive.
   ☐ b. shy and utterly timid.
   ☐ c. a menace to mankind.
   ☐ d. a predictable and uninteresting creature.

3. Meshed beaches are found in
   ☐ a. Africa.
   ☐ b. North America.
   ☐ c. Europe and Asia.
   ☐ d. Australia and South America.

4. We can guess that sharks are
   ☐ a. unpredictable.
   ☐ b. calm and gentle.
   ☐ c. easily repelled.
   ☐ d. defenseless.

5. The second paragraph discusses
   ☐ a. shark fisheries.
   ☐ b. shark repellents.
   ☐ c. meshed beaches.
   ☐ d. the fishing industry.

6. Another word for menace is
   ☐ a. food.
   ☐ b. program.
   ☐ c. serviceman.
   ☐ d. danger.

CATEGORIES OF COMPREHENSION QUESTIONS
No. 1: Subject Matter   No. 3: Supporting Details   No. 5: Clarifying Devices
No. 2: Main Idea   No. 4: Conclusion   No. 6: Vocabulary in Context

---

8. HONKER

In October, nearly three million Canada geese scatter across the length and breadth of the northern two-thirds of North America and begin their majestic migration southward. The big birds, more than a third of them young-of-the-year, now join in loose flocks for southerly flights which will capture the attention of bird watchers, naturalists and hunters for months to come.

This attraction is understandable, for the Canada goose is among the best-known wild birds in America. Millions of us regard its flights in familiar "V" formation as a signal of the coming of autumn, and in spring the honking cry of the wild Canada goose provides a romantic, faraway thrill for even the most apathetic spectator.

Because of its size and intelligence, the Canada goose is also regarded as the number one waterfowl — the big game of waterfowl hunting. This top ranking, particularly among the hunting fraternity, is quite possibly what keeps the Canada goose in such good health today.

Because 3 million geese start south and because there is enough food in the wintering grounds for only 1-1/2 million, the Canada goose season allows hunters to harvest the other half. The 1-1/2 million geese that do reach the wintering grounds are the largest number the food supply can support in a healthy condition. If the geese were not hunted, hundreds of thousands of them would die of starvation or be unable to survive the next spring migration.

Canadas are essentially grazing birds. They feed on a wide variety of plants — all the domestic grains (sometimes incurring the wrath of farmers when they strip young, green grain fields), cord grass, bulrush, salt grass, Bermuda grass, brome grass, clover, alfalfa, eel grass, sea lettuce, pondweed, and many more.

1. A good title for this selection would be
   □ a. The Migration of the Canada Goose.
   □ b. What To Do with a Canada Goose.
   □ c. Be Careful, You Might Cook Your Goose.
   □ d. The History of the Canada Goose.

2. The main thought of this passage is that the Canada goose
   □ a. is highly intelligent.
   □ b. cannot fly long distances.
   □ c. flies south in October.
   □ d. is very healthy.

3. Each year hunters kill about
   □ a. 3,000 geese.
   □ b. 100,000 geese.
   □ c. 1-1/2 million geese.
   □ d. 3 million geese.

4. We can guess that in the spring Canada geese
   □ a. begin to store food.
   □ b. fly northward.
   □ c. become very quarrelsome.
   □ d. migrate further south.

5. The Canada goose is among the best-known wild birds in America. This means that many people
   □ a. are aware of its existence.
   □ b. feel it is a nourishing meal.
   □ c. have been able to tame it.
   □ d. are angered by its mischievous nature.

6. An apathetic spectator is
   □ a. enthusiastic.   □ c. uninterested.
   □ b. well educated.   □ d. extremely nervous.

CATEGORIES OF COMPREHENSION QUESTIONS

No. 1: Subject Matter	No. 3: Supporting Details	No. 5: Clarifying Devices
No. 2: Main Idea	No. 4: Conclusion	No. 6: Vocabulary in Context

9. THE FLIGHT NORTH

As spring approaches, two-year-olds begin to pair up, though it will generally be another year before they nest. Older geese who have lost a mate will search for a new one. Once Canadas mate, they are mated until one is lost.

The Canada goose is a ritualistic bird. If something is worth doing, it is worth a ceremony. Spring finds ganders fighting angrily — they whack each other with their powerful wings and deliver sharp pinches with their beaks. The first to back off is the loser.

Instead of shyly accepting the winner, however, the female demands wooing, and the victor in battle does his best to impress her. Weaving his neck in snakelike motions, head low and bill open, he hisses repeatedly and rustles his puffed-out plumage. If she approves, she may show her feelings by copying his performance. They approach each other, sometimes touching necks, and all is calm. Then they announce their match to the flock by honking at the losing gander and snorting at each other. Finally, they take flight together. A similar ritual accompanies mating, which always takes place on water.

Beginning in early March, Canadas generally follow spring northward, moving into an area when temperatures there reach 35°F. Flying in the familiar "Vs" at speeds between 30 and 60 miles an hour, they move north easily. The lead bird, which changes quite often and may be male or female, breaks the air, stirring updrafts off its wingtips. Following birds ride these updrafts slightly to the outside and, in so doing, increase their flight range 70 percent, according to some scientists. Flying on the updrafts simply requires less effort. In addition, the position allows each goose to see ahead.

Lead birds change often because they get tired, not because of an upset in the social order. However, there *is* an important form of control, more physical than social, in the "V." Birds stay evenly spaced in flight because being out of line on the updrafts increases the work load.

1. This passage mostly discusses the
   ☐ a. ways a Canada goose protects itself.
   ☐ b. mating habits and migration of Canadas.
   ☐ c. various species of geese.
   ☐ d. Canada goose and its young.

2. The Canada goose has
   ☐ a. certain rituals and habits.
   ☐ b. anywhere from three to four mates at one time.
   ☐ c. a very short neck compared to other geese.
   ☐ d. a well-hidden and well-protected nest.

3. Canadas migrate northward in the
   ☐ a. summer.
   ☐ b. fall.
   ☐ c. winter.
   ☐ d. spring.

4. We can conclude that Canadas mate when they are
   ☐ a. three years old.
   ☐ b. four years old.
   ☐ c. five years old.
   ☐ d. six years old.

5. During the springtime the ganders can become
   ☐ a. quite lazy.
   ☐ b. very violent.
   ☐ c. dormant.
   ☐ d. quiet and calm.

6. When a gander makes an effort to impress the female, he is trying
   ☐ a. to pick a fight with her.
   ☐ b. to overpower her so he can be boss.
   ☐ c. to get rid of his mate.
   ☐ d. to get her interested in him.

CATEGORIES OF COMPREHENSION QUESTIONS

No. 1: Subject Matter	No. 3: Supporting Details	No. 5: Clarifying Devices
No. 2: Main Idea	No. 4: Conclusion	No. 6: Vocabulary in Context

The gander and the goose are both devoted to their young. To guard against crowded nesting conditions, the gander chooses and defends a definite territory. The size may depend on height of surrounding vegetation, food supply and amount of visibility from the nest. While Canada geese have been observed nesting twelve to thirty nests per acre, one pair in Utah defended 35 acres of short grass.

Nests are usually on high ground and are built quickly by the female from loose sticks and grass at hand. Later, after laying from two to twelve eggs, she adds down plucked from her breast to make a "blanket" which provides both warmth and camouflage.

The female handles all incubation which lasts twenty-five to twenty-eight days. The male stays nearby to protect her. Protection continues after the young are hatched, and the family moves to a general brooding area — usually a day or two after hatching. Goslings hatch fully covered with down and with eyes open. They are able to hunt for food as soon as they dry.

Compared to mammals, birds attain adult weight much earlier. Young Canadas eat almost continuously and develop rapidly on a basically vegetarian diet. After eight weeks, goslings weigh approximately twenty-four times their birth weight. They can fly at about 2-1/2 months and are ready for the difficult southward migration at about three months. Some eggs never hatch, predators eat many and some goslings are lost. Only about 60 percent escape these dangers and reach maturity.

Though Canada geese may live twenty to thirty years, the average is less than two years. Hunting pressure appears to be the principal reason for this high mortality. However, through closely controlled hunting and good management practices, populations are rising.

I know of no more stirring sight than undulating skeins of Canada geese against the red sky of a frosty fall morning. No matter what I'm doing, I stop to watch and listen as they talk their way southward in their timeless, reassuring flight toward the sun.

1. This passage focuses on the
    ☐ a. use of Canada geese as warning signals.
    ☐ b. nesting habits of Canada geese.
    ☐ c. migratory patterns of Canada geese.
    ☐ d. breeding of Canada geese in captivity.

2. The main thought of this passage is that
    ☐ a. goslings can fly at 2-1/2 months.
    ☐ b. the gander and goose are devoted parents.
    ☐ c. the female goose lines the nest with down.
    ☐ d. the gander chooses the nesting territory.

3. The incubation period for Canada geese is
    ☐ a. ten to twelve days.
    ☐ b. fifteen to twenty days.
    ☐ c. twenty-five to twenty-eight days.
    ☐ d. thirty-five to forty days.

4. The author hints that
    ☐ a. birds grow faster than mammals.
    ☐ b. newborn geese are blind at birth.
    ☐ c. Canada geese eat mostly fish.
    ☐ d. mammals and birds do not get along.

5. A frosty fall morning can be described as
    ☐ a. humid and warm.
    ☐ b. windy and hot.
    ☐ c. dry and sunny.
    ☐ d. chilly and crisp.

6. As used in this selection, maturity means
    ☐ a. management.
    ☐ b. population.
    ☐ c. adulthood.
    ☐ d. brooding.

CATEGORIES OF COMPREHENSION QUESTIONS		
No. 1: Subject Matter	No. 3: Supporting Details	No. 5: Clarifying Devices
No. 2: Main Idea	No. 4: Conclusion	No. 6: Vocabulary in Context

11. GUARDIANS OF THE FOREST

How's this description for the villain of a late-late horror show: a round, barb-tipped tongue nearly twice as long as the head; spine-tipped tail feathers; strong-clawed feet with two toes pointing forward and two backward; a sharp, chisel-like beak; and a muscle and bone structure powerful enough to drill thousands of holes in the hardest wood or, in some cases, rip out fist-size chunks.

This is no science-fiction creation; just a short description of the some-times shy, sometimes gregarious, sometimes loved, sometimes hated woodpecker family — guardians of our forests and probably one of nature's most specialized birds.

As the name implies, woodpeckers have their own way of gathering food. Feeding mainly on wood-boring grubs, insects and insects' eggs and pupae under tree bark and in the wood, woodpeckers are of definite economic importance. Their value is heightened because most of them migrate little or not at all and thus are a year 'round pest control.

Woodpeckers can locate hidden grubs and insects and, because of their highly adapted physical construction, can easily bore holes directly to the prey. Even in winter they have little difficulty locating hibernating insects.

Granted, woodpeckers punch holes in trees, but rarely in a healthy one. When they find a tree infested with wood-boring insects, they locate and devour every pest. Ants which take over abandoned burrows are soon found and devoured, too.

But woodpecker numbers are decreasing, and man is the major reason. With axe, saw, fire prevention programs and insecticides he has destroyed prime woodpecker habitat.

Forest fires and wood-boring insects formerly killed enough trees for large populations of woodpeckers to feed and nest in. The birds in turn fed heavily on insects. However, economic and safety aspects of fire prevention largely ended the creation of habitat through burning. Insecticides kept trees alive and also removed a food staple. So — few dead trees, few insects, few woodpeckers.

1. This article discusses the woodpecker's
   ☐ a. mating habits.
   ☐ b. natural environment.
   ☐ c. flight patterns.
   ☐ d. overpopulation.

2. Woodpeckers are
   ☐ a. multiplying very rapidly.
   ☐ b. quarrelsome, dangerous creatures.
   ☐ c. valuable birds.
   ☐ d. of little economic value.

3. Woodpeckers feed mostly on
   ☐ a. the eggs of reptiles.
   ☐ b. the seeds of conifers.
   ☐ c. wood-boring insects.
   ☐ d. wild berries.

4. We can conclude that woodpeckers
   ☐ a. are very devoted parents to their young.
   ☐ b. will attack other birds.
   ☐ c. often live in empty burrows on the ground.
   ☐ d. find their food in diseased or dead trees.

5. The first paragraph talks about the woodpecker's
   ☐ a. easy-going nature.
   ☐ b. nesting habits.
   ☐ c. physical appearance.
   ☐ d. diet.

6. A gregarious bird
   ☐ a. has difficulty flying.
   ☐ b. migrates south for the winter.
   ☐ c. does not mate for life.
   ☐ d. is found in groups.

CATEGORIES OF COMPREHENSION QUESTIONS

No. 1: Subject Matter   No. 3: Supporting Details   No. 5: Clarifying Devices
No. 2: Main Idea   No. 4: Conclusion   No. 6: Vocabulary in Context

12. WOOD IS STILL WOOD TO A WOODPECKER

Woodpeckers have been around a long time, about 25 million years. This long history has given them time to populate nearly every reach of the globe and to evolve into the specialists they are today. In the United States alone, forty-five species and sub-species can be seen — or heard — combing the forests for insect food.

The woodpecker family includes the flickers and sapsuckers and has cousins in the desert, in alpine forests, in hardwood forests, in swamps, in backyard woodlots, in big timber, little timber, cacti and even in telephone poles.

Yet, specialized as the body structure and feeding habits of the family have become, a group this large and widespread also has eccentrics and variations on the woodpecker theme. Sometimes these variations go too far, as far as man is concerned.

The yellow-bellied sapsucker, for instance, drills rows of holes in healthy trees, often killing them. He then laps up the oozing sap with a short, brush-tipped tongue — a variation on the woodpecker-type tongue. This most migratory member of the woodpecker clan offsets his damage by feeding heavily on insects, too.

Some woodpeckers — particularly the pileated — have been quite destructive to telephone and electricity poles. Utility companies have tried painting poles odd colors, wrapping wire around poles, brushing poles with foul-tasting mixtures — everything short of metal poles or metal sheaths for wooden poles. Nothing works; wood is still wood to a woodpecker.

Other woodpeckers have become fond of fruit and grain crops, particularly when insects are in short supply. This taste has also gotten them in trouble.

Woodpeckers appear to be constantly hungry, for they never seem to pause long in their search for insects. With spiny tail feathers braced against a tree trunk and claws solidly anchored in the wood, they pry and chisel into bark and inner wood, into rotten logs or even into sap houses.

1. Choose the best title.
   - ☐ a. The Destructive Woodpecker
   - ☐ b. Woodpecker Fossils
   - ☐ c. Extinction of the Pileated Woodpecker
   - ☐ d. Woodpeckers for Sale

2. The main idea of this article is that
   - ☐ a. some woodpeckers live in cacti.
   - ☐ b. the woodpecker is a migratory bird.
   - ☐ c. woodpeckers are slowly becoming extinct.
   - ☐ d. there are many variations of woodpeckers.

3. The yellow-bellied sapsucker feeds on
   - ☐ a. seeds.
   - ☐ b. evergreen leaves.
   - ☐ c. sap.
   - ☐ d. parasites.

4. Woodpeckers
   - ☐ a. live only in hardwood forests.
   - ☐ b. are found all over the world.
   - ☐ c. have a very delicate structure.
   - ☐ d. help to pollinate plants.

5. The author mentions the pileated woodpecker to show that woodpeckers
   - ☐ a. are easily trained.
   - ☐ b. can cause extensive damage.
   - ☐ c. often migrate southward.
   - ☐ d. avoid any contact with humans.

6. Oozing sap flows
   - ☐ a. erratically.
   - ☐ b. upward.
   - ☐ c. slowly.
   - ☐ d. swiftly.

CATEGORIES OF COMPREHENSION QUESTIONS

No. 1: Subject Matter	No. 3: Supporting Details	No. 5: Clarifying Devices
No. 2: Main Idea	No. 4: Conclusion	No. 6: Vocabulary in Context

13. WOODPECKERS

Courtship and nesting habits are essentially alike in all woodpeckers. Much of the rivalry between males is confined to pursuit, with little combat taking place.

The pileated, however, is a battler. He will not tolerate another male anywhere in his territory. His penetrating call is a signal for males with matrimony on their mind to prepare for battle. With crest erect and wings held stiffly at his side, the male first tries to scare intruders away. If this fails, he will fight fiercely.

Woodpeckers usually lay three to eight eggs, generally in a hollowed-out nest in a dead or dying tree. The eggs are white, as they are in most cavity-dwelling birds. The Gila woodpecker, a resident of the southwestern deserts, generally pecks out a nest in the giant saguaro cactus. The red-headed woodpecker sometimes carves a hole in a telephone pole or fence post, but more often in a big oak tree. The red cockaded always drills its nest in a living pine tree that has a dead heart.

Most woodpeckers know how the family should act, particularly in food gathering habits. Not the flicker. He spends most of his time feeding on the ground. Though he stumbles across your lawn on short, weak legs, his slightly curved bill and smooth, sticky tongue (both characteristics unlike other woodpeckers) make his bumbling frolics a successful hunt, particularly for ants, where the sticky tongue does yeoman sweeping service.

Like the flicker, the red-headed woodpecker often disdains the peck-and-pry method. From his perch on a dead tree or stub, he leaps to capture insects on the wing or on the ground. He flutters through the air more like a flycatcher, returning to his perch to eat his catch.

1. This article tells mostly about
   - □ a. the different habits of woodpeckers.
   - □ b. the woodpecker's physical appearance.
   - □ c. care of young woodpeckers.
   - □ d. the Gila woodpecker.

2. The courtship and nesting habits among woodpeckers
   - □ a. differ greatly.
   - □ b. are never seen by humans.
   - □ c. are basically the same.
   - □ d. resemble the mating habits of other birds.

3. Woodpecker eggs are
   - □ a. white.
   - □ b. yellow.
   - □ c. blue.
   - □ d. pink.

4. After reading this passage, we can see that most of the time woodpeckers nest
   - □ a. on the branches of dead trees.
   - □ b. inside large trees or plants.
   - □ c. in rock shelters.
   - □ d. in hollowed-out furrows on the ground.

5. When the flicker searches for food, he looks
   - □ a. comical.
   - □ b. sad.
   - □ c. serious.
   - □ d. graceful.

6. As used in this passage, pursuit means
   - □ a. fight.
   - □ c. nesting.
   - □ b. capture.
   - □ d. chase.

CATEGORIES OF COMPREHENSION QUESTIONS

No. 1: Subject Matter	No. 3: Supporting Details	No. 5: Clarifying Devices
No. 2: Main Idea	No. 4: Conclusion	No. 6: Vocabulary in Context

14. THE GREAT IVORY-BILLED WOODPECKER

The biggest woodpecker ever known on North America was — or perhaps is — the ivory-billed. Similar to the smaller pileated, but distinguished easily by the white feathers on the back of its wings, the ivory-bill was once common in the forest of the southeast. Unable to live in logged-over forests, however, they disappeared gradually until, by the end of World War II, they were either the rarest American bird or the most recently extinct.

Now, however, researcher John Dennis has found evidence of between five and ten pairs of ivory-bills deep in the Neches River Valley in the "Big Thicket" country of southeast Texas. He pointed out that, if they could remain hidden in those woods for sixty-two years, they can continue to live and even multiply with proper management and protection.

Rare, indeed; endangered, certainly; but extinct, probably not. The ivory-bill may still survive.

Woodpeckers are basically less migratory than other birds. The majority will occupy the same area throughout the year. The yellow-bellied sapsucker, however, winters in the Gulf states and returns in the spring to drill out sap holes in birch and maple trees in the East. The yellow-shafted flicker leaves his northern range for sections where an ample ant supply is available. The Arizona woodpecker and the red-naped sapsucker spend their respective summers in highlands and migrate to lower levels during the winter.

The end of fall and beginning of winter brings a prolonged hush over a brooding landscape. But a pileated or a downy or a red-headed or most any member of the clan will suddenly shatter the silence with a staccato beat. Those who hear the pounding will warm to the knowledge that a woodpecker is still at work — solitary, often thankless, but dignified — resolutely carrying out his task as guardian of the forest.

1. This passage centers mostly on
   ☐ a. the great ivory-billed woodpecker.
   ☐ b. the downy woodpecker.
   ☐ c. the flicker.
   ☐ d. the pileated woodpecker.

2. The writer's main idea is
   ☐ a. to show how disorganized the woodpecker can be.
   ☐ b. to point out the nesting habits of woodpeckers.
   ☐ c. to explain migratory patterns of woodpeckers.
   ☐ d. to present many facts about woodpeckers.

3. According to this article, when compared to other species of birds, the woodpecker is
   ☐ a. much smaller.   ☐ c. not as abundant.
   ☐ b. less migratory.   ☐ d. not as intelligent.

4. We can guess that naturalists
   ☐ a. are not interested in the habits of woodpeckers.
   ☐ b. are not always aware of the existence of some animals.
   ☐ c. are studying the loud sounds that woodpeckers make.
   ☐ d. are afraid that the flicker is now extinct.

5. To "shatter the silence" means
   ☐ a. to drop something soft.
   ☐ b. to be very quiet and still.
   ☐ c. to awaken from a peaceful sleep.
   ☐ d. to make noise.

6. An ample supply is
   ☐ a. a winter supply.
   ☐ b. a large supply.
   ☐ c. an ancient supply.
   ☐ d. a limited supply.

CATEGORIES OF COMPREHENSION QUESTIONS

| No. 1: Subject Matter | No. 3: Supporting Details | No. 5: Clarifying Devices |
| No. 2: Main Idea | No. 4: Conclusion | No. 6: Vocabulary in Context |

15. THE OCTOPUS'S SOULFUL EYE

The octopus is an eight-tentacled creature with a head that is all beak and soulful eyes. It is found everywhere there are foaming seas and bouldered shores, but particularly on our Pacific Coast and in the Florida Keys.

Most of the 140 species are less than 3 feet across and this includes a generous expanse of spindly arm. Some tiny octopuses — or octopii, if you prefer — are full-grown at 1/2 inch. One species in the Pacific grows to 28 feet. Tall tales of larger octopuses are probably the result of our mistaking the creature for the squid.

Those soulful eyes we mentioned earlier are strangely human, and they are one of the more striking physical characteristics of the octopus. The eyes are as highly developed as our own and are the thing that bothers people most about the octopus. "It's not the looks of the octopus," one fisherman told us with a shudder. "It's the way the octopus looks." The eyes of the octopus register all shades of emotion. They can be as gentle as the eyes of the human mother when caring for their young; they can blaze with eagerness when seeking a mate; they can glow with rage when danger threatens.

When it is attacked, the octopus emits a stream of inky fluid in the direction of its pursuers, while jet-propelling itself with incredible speed in another direction. The ink is harmless; it has no effect on human skin or upon fishes. At one time it was thought to be a clever smoke screen behind which the octopus could flee to shelter. The emission of pigment into the water however is too small to conceal the octopus. What then is the purpose of the ink barrage? An interesting explanation is that the bomb of ink emitted by the octopus is shaped exactly like the octopus itself and is of about the same size. Therefore, the so-called smoke screen may be a ruse to divert weak-eyed enemies or pursuers. Scientists have noted that the ink appears to paralyze the sense of smell of the most persistent enemy of the octopus, the deadly moray eel. And this indeed could be its purpose since in various experiments, the eel appeared to be completely oblivious to the presence of the octopus after a squirting.

1. This selection mainly talks about the octupus's
   - □ a. diet and mating rituals.
   - □ b. physical appearance and survival habits.
   - □ c. natural environment.
   - □ d. nature and extinction.

2. The octopus is mostly found in
   - □ a. cold, arctic or subarctic regions.
   - □ b. the Pacific and Florida Keys.
   - □ c. the Sea of Japan.
   - □ d. the deepest waters of the Atlantic Ocean.

3. How many tentacles does the octopus have?
   - □ a. Five
   - □ b. Eight
   - □ c. Ten
   - □ d. Twelve

4. A natural enemy of the octopus is the
   - □ a. moray eel.
   - □ b. giant squid.
   - □ c. blue whale.
   - □ d. sand shark.

5. A weak-eyed enemy
   - □ a. does not have eyes.
   - □ b. cannot see underwater.
   - □ c. does not see well.
   - □ d. is totally blind.

6. A ruse is
   - □ a. an enemy.
   - □ b. a trick.
   - □ c. a food.
   - □ d. an acid.

CATEGORIES OF COMPREHENSION QUESTIONS

No. 1: Subject Matter   No. 3: Supporting Details   No. 5: Clarifying Devices
No. 2: Main Idea   No. 4: Conclusion   No. 6: Vocabulary in Context

16. THE REAL MR. OCTOPUS

The octopus has a completely unjustified reputation for frightfulness. It is a timid, nocturnal creature who would rather flee than face anything larger than itself. It uses its parrotlike beak for cutting food and for defense, but it has never been known to have bitten a human being, let alone kill anyone.

Some of the vilification of the octopus is due to its being confused with the less docile squid to which it is related. Squids swim around in large schools (the octopus stays put) and will bite when caught or bothered. A squid may measure from 1-1/2 inches to 50 feet across. The giant squid is undoubtedly the source of the octopus terror talk. A few years ago a tremendous whale was harpooned and in its belly was found tentacles 50 feet long. This would make the devoured creature, probably a giant squid, at least 110 feet across! Such giant squids are believed to exist in the depths of the Pacific.

The octopus has two mortal enemies: the moray eel and . . . man. In parts of the world where the octopus is regarded as a gastronomic delicacy, it is in danger of extermination. We Americans evidence only a minor interest in the octopus as an article of food, so our coasts are teeming with the creatures.

The fertility of the octopus is a big factor in combating its high mortality. The female will lay as many as 45,000 pearly-white eggs about the size of a half-grain of rice, which she drapes from rocks in long necklaces. During the incubation period, about 6 to 8 weeks, the mother eats no food. From time to time she will squirt the eggs with water to keep them clean, and she will drive off any octopus which might approach. When the babies hatch, the mother crawls off and dies. The baby octopuses have all the helpless appeal of other newborn creatures. Waving tiny tentacles in an ineffectual challenge, they stare wide-eyed, with their near human eyes, at a frightening, hostile world.

1. This article mostly discusses the octopus's
   □ a. dietary habits.
   □ b. destructive and harmful nature.
   □ c. fearsome predation tendencies.
   □ d. reputation and near extinction.

2. The octopus is
   □ a. ill-tempered.
   □ b. timid.
   □ c. courageous.
   □ d. aggressive.

3. According to this passage, the octopus is related to the
   □ a. clam.
   □ b. starfish.
   □ c. squid.
   □ d. crab.

4. In some parts of the world the octopus is
   □ a. being overhunted.
   □ b. terribly diseased.
   □ c. very small in size.
   □ d. developing a tougher skin.

5. A parrot and an octopus are alike because both of them
   □ a. are a greenish color.
   □ b. have similar beaks.
   □ c. make the same sound.
   □ d. have claws.

6. A hostile world is
   □ a. fruitful.
   □ b. organized.
   □ c. unfriendly.
   □ d. efficient.

CATEGORIES OF COMPREHENSION QUESTIONS

No. 1: Subject Matter   No. 3: Supporting Details   No. 5: Clarifying Devices
No. 2: Main Idea   No. 4: Conclusion   No. 6: Vocabulary in Context

17. HUNGRY GANGSTER OF THE DEEP

The starfish's chief task in life is to eat — at times almost continuously, though the feeding rate varies considerably with age, water temperature, food availability and other factors. Picture, for example, his attack on an oyster. "Tortures" would really be a better word, for the process takes hours. Though the star has five eyes, one at the end of each arm, and possesses one of the most complex nervous systems among the invertebrates, its sense organs are poorly developed. Since he lacks any ability to sense the presence of food at any great distance, the starfish sometimes has to literally stumble upon its prey by accident. Having chanced upon a young oyster, he clenches it in his arms, blanketing it with the numerous sucker-feet on the undersides of his arms. He then tries to straighten his arms in opposite directions to open the oyster, exerting a pull of as much as 12 pounds. He is not strong enough to accomplish the task immediately, but his prey cannot overcome even a weak pull for a long period and soon surrenders.

Because his mouth is only one-fourth inch in diameter, the starfish cannot take in large pieces of food. He, therefore, practices a unique method of feeding. He eats with his stomach, which he can push out through the mouth centrally located beneath his body. Inserting his inside-out stomach into the oyster shell through an opening which may be only 1/25 inch wide, the star proceeds to digest the soft oyster meat on the spot.

The starfish can digest an oyster without even coming in contact with its flesh, for a star's digestive enzyme is so strong it can function effectively even after being diluted in seawater and oyster juice. The star literally digests an oyster alive, devouring the tissue while the bivalve's heart still beats. After this is done, the starfish simply withdraws its stomach to its normal position within the body cavity. One starfish can finish off about six young oysters a day by this incredible process.

1. This article mostly discusses the starfish's
   □ a. mating habits.
   □ b. sense organs.
   □ c. feeding habits.
   □ d. nervous system.

2. The best statement of the main idea of this passage is that
   □ a. the starfish's main purpose in life is to find food.
   □ b. the starfish has five eyes at the end of each arm.
   □ c. fishermen find the starfish a bothersome creature.
   □ d. the nervous system of the starfish is very complex.

3. The starfish's mouth is only
   □ a. 1/25 inch wide.
   □ b. 1/12 inch across.
   □ c. 1/4 inch in diameter.
   □ d. 1/2 inch wide.

4. Starfish seem to feed on
   □ a. shellfish.
   □ b. seaworms.
   □ c. algae.
   □ d. plankton.

5. A starfish blankets its prey. This means the starfish
   □ a. ignores its prey.
   □ b. gets on top of its prey.
   □ c. paralyzes its prey.
   □ d. kills its prey by heating it.

6. Another word for task is
   □ a. food.
   □ b. prey.
   □ c. diet.
   □ d. job.

CATEGORIES OF COMPREHENSION QUESTIONS

No. 1: Subject Matter	No. 3: Supporting Details	No. 5: Clarifying Devices
No. 2: Main Idea	No. 4: Conclusion	No. 6: Vocabulary in Context

18. THE COMMON STARFISH

A starfish, like most of its relatives, is born of parents whose sex usually cannot be discovered except by microscopic examination. Spawning takes place in warm water from May to July, the female discharging thousands of eggs into the water, where they are immediately fertilized by the male. The eggs hatch after about twenty-four hours into <u>minute</u> organisms roughly one-tenth the size of a pinhead. These organisms increase about fifty times in size within the next three weeks and then begin to assume their star shapes.

Normally, adult stars have five arms, but they can possess as many as forty-four, and they range in size from 1/2 inch to more than 3 feet across. All stars have a single opening on the central disc through which water passes in and out of the body.

The common star is found in waters from Maine to Florida and the Gulf of Mexico. It cannot migrate far from its birthplace since it travels at the rate of only 3 to 6 inches a minute, or from 2 to 4 miles a month.

Eating its fill and taking life easy on the bottom, the starfish seems to have no problems. But the starfish has its natural enemies, too, and except for the spiny armor of its external skeleton is completely defenseless against them. Their enemies include gulls, ravens, crows and foxes — all of them capable of catching the star when it is trapped in shallow tide pools. Parasites eat away parts of its body, but luckily for him he has the ability to regrow new body parts that have been destroyed or injured.

A starfish wounded in a fight has the ability to cast off an arm whenever he desires. Not only can he grow a new arm when he loses one, but an entire body will be regenerated if the arm separated from his body contains a portion of the central disc. With regenerative ability like this, it seems certain that he will continue to plague fishermen for many years to come and retain its richly deserved title as the walking stomach of the sea.

1. Select the best title for this article.
   ☐ a. Experiments with Starfish
   ☐ b. Let's Discuss the Starfish
   ☐ c. The Starfish's Keen Eyesight
   ☐ d. The Fastest Fish of the Sea

2. The writer's main idea is
   ☐ a. to present many facts about starfish.
   ☐ b. to show how starfish migrate.
   ☐ c. to explain the economic value of starfish.
   ☐ d. to describe the starfish's five senses.

3. The starfish can travel
   ☐ a. 2 to 4 miles a month.
   ☐ b. 5 to 10 miles a month.
   ☐ c. 12 to 15 miles a month.
   ☐ d. 20 to 24 miles a month.

4. After reading this passage, we can guess that
   ☐ a. starfish don't have any enemies.
   ☐ b. fishermen dislike the starfish.
   ☐ c. scientists are finding more ways to use the starfish.
   ☐ d. the starfish is a parasite.

5. The first paragraph talks about
   ☐ a. the central disc of the starfish.
   ☐ b. the starfish's natural enemies.
   ☐ c. regenerative abilities of the starfish.
   ☐ d. reproduction of the starfish.

6. Starfish eggs hatch into <u>minute</u> organisms. This means that the young
   starfish are
   ☐ a. helpless.   ☐ c. hungry.
   ☐ b. very small.   ☐ d. large.

CATEGORIES OF COMPREHENSION QUESTIONS

No. 1: Subject Matter   No. 3: Supporting Details   No. 5: Clarifying Devices
No. 2: Main Idea   No. 4: Conclusion   No. 6: Vocabulary in Context

---

19. NATURE'S DEADLINESS

There are over 300,000 different kinds of plants. At least 700 of them are poisonous. Poisonous plants are all around in field and forest, desert and pond, park and roadside, home and office. No rule of geography, habitat, color, size, relationship, or anything else exists to help learn them, and only one rule, if enforced, can absolutely prevent poisoning. Don't eat anything you do not know to be good, wholesome, fresh or properly preserved food.

Here are a few facts about some plants. Common field buttercups produce sap that changes rapidly into an irritant substance when the plant is killed. It can cause burns on tender skin or severe digestive upset if eaten in quantity.

Everyone knows that apples are wholesome and desirable in the regular diet. Few realize that, in common with many of their close relatives in the rose family, they concentrate cyanide in their seeds. A few seeds are harmless because cyanide is readily eliminated by the body and quite a bit must be present before any harmful effects occur. The difference between a harmless amount and a deadly amount is sharp. If you are poisoned at all, you are likely to die unless treatment is prompt and effective. A cupful of apple seeds saved up by a person who thinks them a delicacy to be eaten all at once would be fatal.

The pits (seeds) of some peaches, cherries and apricots and the foliage and bark of many of the wild cherries can do the same, but this danger is mostly to animals because people don't eat quantities of any of these things.

One of the most dangerous plants containing a digitalislike drug is oleander. A few leaves of this plant can kill a human being. Repeatedly, persons have been poisoned by meat roasted on sticks cut from oleander shrubs over a backyard fire. It's really a good idea to know a little bit more about nature's deadly storehouse.

1. This article tells about
   - ☐ a. herbs and spices.
   - ☐ b. insect-eating plants.
   - ☐ c. plants used in medicine.
   - ☐ d. poisonous plants.

2. Choose the main idea of this selection.
   - ☐ a. Some plants are harmful.
   - ☐ b. The forest floor is a storehouse of herbs.
   - ☐ c. Mushrooms can be poisonous.
   - ☐ d. Some plants get nitrogen from insects.

3. Apple seeds contain
   - ☐ a. strychnine.
   - ☐ b. cyanide.
   - ☐ c. digitalis
   - ☐ d. arsenic.

4. Which of the following is most likely true?
   - ☐ a. Most of the plants in the northern hemisphere are edible.
   - ☐ b. Campers know which plants to avoid.
   - ☐ c. Many plants make their own medicine.
   - ☐ d. Some members of the rose family contain poisonous parts.

5. Oleander is a
   - ☐ a. type of fern.
   - ☐ b. short, bushlike plant.
   - ☐ c. tall hardwood tree.
   - ☐ d. winding vine.

6. A good synonym for prompt is
   - ☐ a. delicate.
   - ☐ b. slow.
   - ☐ c. quick.
   - ☐ d. careful.

CATEGORIES OF COMPREHENSION QUESTIONS

No. 1: Subject Matter	No. 3: Supporting Details	No. 5: Clarifying Devices
No. 2: Main Idea	No. 4: Conclusion	No. 6: Vocabulary in Context

20. BEAUTIFUL BUT DEADLY

Poisonous plants around the house are more common than you think. Japanese yew is one of the commonest elements of foundation plantings around homes. Its needlelike foliage contains an alkaloid which abruptly stops the heart. Despite the attractiveness of its flowers, the bulbs of the Star of Bethlehem are rapidly lethal in small amounts.

Some plants cause chronic poisoning. Oak (any part, including acorns) causes damage to develop slowly in the kidneys. Horsechestnuts, and the foliage of the tree, are also poisonous. Labratory experiments have shown that the sweet pea (the flower) produces skeletal deformity and a nervous condition in laboratory animals.

You can find wisteria vine on the porch of one or many houses in nearly every town throughout much of the United States. Yet, before 1961, it had never been reported as poisonous in this country. Now, many cases of severe digestive upset and hospitalization of children who ate its seeds or pods are on record.

Rhododendrons contain an irritant substance which causes severe vomiting if eaten. In more than small amounts they can cause death. The part of the rhubarb plant which is eaten is the stalk (petiole) of the leaf. It owes its taste to certain organic acids which are entirely harmless. For some reason, however, the blade of the leaf contains oxalic acid and is lethal.

One or two seeds of the castor bean or the rosary pea can be lethal under some circumstances. Necklaces made of these seeds are found in homes throughout the country. They are dangerous around children and should be destroyed.

The best defense is knowlege and good practice. Keep younger children away from poisonous plants. Educate older children so you can rely on them never to eat unknown plants.

1. What is the subject of this article?
   - ☐ a. Common deadly plants
   - ☐ b. Useful shrubs
   - ☐ c. Good garden plants
   - ☐ d. Greenhouses and their plants

2. The main idea of this selection is that
   - ☐ a. many of our common shrubs are hybrids.
   - ☐ b. garden plants need a lot of care.
   - ☐ c. most plants grow better in a greenhouse.
   - ☐ d. some plants found around the home are lethal.

3. The rhubarb leaf contains
   - ☐ a. vitamin A.
   - ☐ b. oxalic acid.
   - ☐ c. phosphorous.
   - ☐ d. nitric acid.

4. The passage implies that
   - ☐ a. poisonous plants have to be eaten in order to be harmful.
   - ☐ b. rhubarb is a sweet-tasting plant.
   - ☐ c. almost all plant seeds are poisonous.
   - ☐ d. common garden plants grow best in acidy soil.

5. The leaves of the Japanese yew are
   - ☐ a. round, waxy and broad.
   - ☐ b. fat, short and thick.
   - ☐ c. oval and egg shaped.
   - ☐ d. long, slender and pointed.

6. A chronic illness is
   - ☐ a. short lived.
   - ☐ b. not serious.
   - ☐ c. a continuing illness.
   - ☐ d. inherited.

CATEGORIES OF COMPREHENSION QUESTIONS

No. 1: Subject Matter	No. 3: Supporting Details	No. 5: Clarifying Devices
No. 2: Main Idea	No. 4: Conclusion	No. 6: Vocabulary in Context

21. WHAT'S UP FOR WINTER?

The advent of winter calls for a change of clothing for wildlife, as well as for humans. Warmth is the prime requisite, and the natural winter coats of wild animals and birds of the north are warmer for their weight than anything Man has been able to manufacture. Dead air is the miracle insulator; by retaining body heat it makes life possible in even the polar regions.

Winter fur and feathers are designed to achieve this end. The familiar northern white-tailed deer, for example, wears a summer coat of straight, slender hairs. The hairs of the winter coat, on the other hand, are not only stout and crinkled, but hollow as well, each containing its own dead air cell. In addition there is a scanty undercoat of fine wool for added warmth.

In birds, insulation has reached near perfection. Feathers in themselves are amazingly effective air traps. With the addition of a dense layer of down, such birds as the sea ducks and the penguins can be blasé about the coldest temperatures. Because their plumage is waterproofed with secretions of their oil glands, they can swim in near-freezing water with ease.

Birds can also regulate the degree of insulation by compressing their feathers to drive out the trapped air in warmer weather and fluffing them when it's cold.

Some mammals change to a different color in winter. The white-tailed, for example, swaps his summer red for grayish brown. The gray squirrel, whose thin summer coat is generously tinged with brown, assumes a clear gray fur in winter. A few mammals go all the way, donning pure white coats for midwinter to be camouflaged in the snow. The well-known ermine is nothing more than a northern weasel that has replaced its brown summer hairs with white ones.

The varying hare, commonly known as the "snowshoe rabbit," not only turns white in winter, but its huge feet are made even bigger by growing a fringe of stiff hairs that serve as wonderfully effective snowshoes.

1. This passage discusses how animals
   □ a. store food.
   □ b. adapt to winter.
   □ c. seek shelter.
   □ d. feed their young.

2. Winter fur and feathers are designed
   □ a. to repel moisture.
   □ b. to prevent freezing.
   □ c. for easy shedding.
   □ d for warmth.

3. This article tells us that an animal's greatest insulator is
   □ a. body fat.
   □ b. air.
   □ c. oil.
   □ d. the sun.

4. The author hints that, compared to an animal's coat, Man has not been able to create a winter coat that is both
   □ a. insulated and heavy.
   □ b. beautiful and long lasting.
   □ c. warm and lightweight.
   □ d. white and thick.

5. The writer mentions the penguins to show that
   □ a. all birds do not have thick feathers.
   □ b. blubber is a good insulator.
   □ c. some birds are quite adept at handling freezing temperatures.
   □ d. many birds depend upon the sea for their food.

6. A scanty coat of fur is
   □ a. coarse.   □ c. hollow.
   □ b. thick.   □ d. thin.

CATEGORIES OF COMPREHENSION QUESTIONS

No. 1: Subject Matter	No. 3: Supporting Details	No. 5: Clarifying Devices
No. 2: Main Idea	No. 4: Conclusion	No. 6: Vocabulary in Context

22. PERSEVERENCE PAYS

Despite every bar that we civilized Americans have put in their way — pollution, dams, irrigation diversions, logging debris — Pacific salmon, per pound of fish, remain our most valuable fishery resource. True, the catch by our commercial fishermen has dropped from almost 800 million pounds in 1936 to less than 300 million pounds in recent years, but this was to be expected. Spawning runs are being eliminated in river after river, and fishermen from other nations now are taking North American fish in midocean.

The amazing thing is that the salmon have been able to maintain their population as well as they have. They are born in freshwater rivers, drift seaward as fry and fingerlings, mature in saltwater and then — like migratory birds — use the angles of the sun's rays to plot a return course to their natal stream, which they ascend one time to spawn and die.

Remembered temperature and salty currents may guide them homeward. Its sense of smell helps each salmon to recognize the mouth of the river system to which its own stream belongs, causing it to turn upriver and then to take the correct turns all along the upstream journey. Their struggles to reach their upstream spawning beds are awe-inspiring. Investigators measuring the ability and persistence of salmon in ascending fishways traced one sockeye salmon as it ascended an endless fishway for over five days, climbing 6,648 feet before the test was discontinued because of exhaustion of the investigators rather than of the fish.

There are at least six species of Pacific salmon, of which five are native to the northeast Pacific ocean: chum, pink, red or sockeye, silver or coho and chinook or king. The king salmon is king of them all in size (as much as 100 pounds), length of migration (up to 3,000 miles), food quality (its commercial value is highest, up to $1 a pound to the fisherman) and sport fishing qualities (90 percent of all salmon taken on sport fishing tackle are kings or silvers).

As long as man permits its continued existence, the king salmon — a savage striker with a stout heart and tremendous fighting ability — will remain one of North America's most popular fishes.

1. Another good title for this article would be
   □ a. Differences Between Salmon and Tuna.
   □ b. Predator of Our Rivers.
   □ c. Migration of Salmon.
   □ d. Pollution Stopped the Salmon.

2. Salmon
   □ a. return to their native stream to spawn.
   □ b. are considered trash fish in some places.
   □ c. are becoming extinct.
   □ d. have been affected by oil spills.

3. The largest of all salmon is the
   □ a. chinook.
   □ b. chum.
   □ c. pink.
   □ d. sockeye.

4. Salmon seem to be able
   □ a. to fast during migration.
   □ b. to dig very deep mud shelters.
   □ c. to survive very well in captivity.
   □ d. to live in both salt and fresh water.

5. The next to last paragraph discusses the
   □ a. diet of the salmon.
   □ b. different kinds of salmon.
   □ c. mating of the salmon.
   □ d. fish hatcheries.

6. A fry is a
   □ a waterway.
   □ b. baby fish.
   □ c. watersnake.
   □ d. large salmon.

CATEGORIES OF COMPREHENSION QUESTIONS		
No. 1: Subject Matter	No. 3: Supporting Details	No. 5: Clarifying Devices
No. 2: Main Idea	No. 4: Conclusion	No. 6: Vocabulary in Context

23. BOOMING GROUNDS AND THE PRAIRIE CHICKEN

Prairie chickens are best known for their courtship activity — an arena display which occurs on traditional "booming grounds" each spring. A booming or display ground is a small level area of short vegetation. The primary requirement for this display area is good visibility. Courtship postures and movements must be easily seen by other prairie chickens, unobstructed by tall grass or weeds. Birds often choose an elevated site, such as a ridge or knoll. Most birds return to the same booming ground year after year.

In late February, male prairie chickens begin visiting the booming grounds each morning and evening. During the first few weeks, cocks fight among themselves until each has established a territory of his own — just a few square feet of ground which the bird returns to each day and defends against other males.

The cock's striking courtship dance is directed toward rival males, as well as prospective mates. The display frequently begins with a short run. Suddenly the bird stops and stamps his feet very rapidly, often pivoting as he "dances." A brilliantly colored air sac around his neck begins to inflate. The bare flesh on each side of the sac is orange in the greater prairie chicken, rosy-colored in the lesser.

Tail feathers and pinnae (long feathers on each side of his neck) are erected, head and neck are lowered, and a very peculiar sound is produced in the throat and resonated in the air sacs. The greater prairie chicken "booms" — a sound somewhat like air blown across an open bottle top. The call of the lesser prairie chicken has been described as more of a "gobble." The booming or gobbling is a low sound, but it can be heard over a mile away on a still day.

Booming grounds are used until June, when most of the hens are occupied with nesting. Around a dozen eggs are laid in a nest on the ground. Newly-hatched chicks are covered with down and are active within an hour. They stay near the hen but easily catch their own insect food. When four weeks old, the young chickens can fly a short distance. By the age of ten weeks they are ready to leave the hen.

Come fall, prairie chickens return to the booming grounds. Display activities go on until severe weather calls a halt. Fall displays are less intense than those in spring, and no mating occurs. Chickens spend the winter in mixed flocks — males and females grouping together until spring.

1. Select the best title.
   - ☐ a. How To Protect Yourself against Chickens
   - ☐ b. Prairie Chickens on the Move
   - ☐ c. Mating Habits of the Prairie Chicken
   - ☐ d. A Young Chicken Leaves Home

2. Prairie chickens are well-known for their
   - ☐ a. colorful tail feathers.
   - ☐ b. courtship activities.
   - ☐ c. large nests.
   - ☐ d. soft down.

3. At what age do young prairie chickens leave the hen?
   - ☐ a. One week
   - ☐ b. Four weeks
   - ☐ c. Eight weeks
   - ☐ d. Ten weeks

4. The writer hints that prairie chickens feed on
   - ☐ a. insects.
   - ☐ b. plants.
   - ☐ c. carrion.
   - ☐ d. rodents.

5. When the cocks first reach the booming ground, they could be described as
   - ☐ a. lazy.
   - ☐ b. quarrelsome.
   - ☐ c. shy.
   - ☐ d. calm.

6. A rival is
   - ☐ a. a friend.
   - ☐ b. a brother.
   - ☐ c. an enemy.
   - ☐ d. a neighbor.

CATEGORIES OF COMPREHENSION QUESTIONS

No. 1: Subject Matter   No. 3: Supporting Details   No. 5: Clarifying Devices

No. 2: Main Idea   No. 4: Conclusion   No. 6: Vocabulary in Context

24. A HOME AWAY FROM HOME

The big, salt-water, striped bass has for generations lured anglers to New England shores to stand hip-deep in the pounding surf and cast time and again in hopes of hooking a big "rockfish," the prize of a lifetime. The landlocked fishermen a thousand miles inland could never expect to share this magnificent experience without making long trips to the edge of the ocean — never, that is, until recently.

Now, however, this same sea-dwelling striped bass has begun a surprising migration inland, far from his native coastal waters. It is this migration that has anglers in many places looking hopefully to the day when they may catch a 50-pound game fish close to their homes in Little Rock, Nashville, St. Louis and a number of other cities. The strange story of how the rockfish left his salt-water home had its beginning in November of 1941 near the little South Carolina town of Moncks Corner.

Engineers shut the gates on the new Pinopolis Dam, and waters from the Santee and the Cooper Rivers backed up behind the new structure to form two new lakes named Marion and Moultree. The engineers had no way of knowing that they had set the stage for a fish story that would excite anglers and biologists across the country for years to come.

For more years than anyone knows, striped bass swam up the Santee and Cooper Rivers from the Atlantic to spawn. No one was greatly surprised when anglers continued to make good catches of striped bass in the trail-waters below the new dam. They were not even much surprised when isolated catches began being reported from the new lakes. It was quite logical that some of the fish had been trapped behind the dam.

But within a few years, fishermen began reporting schools of *young* striped bass. They happily explored new methods of catching the beautiful, strong, fighting stripers and never worried too long about the fact that the young fish were there at all. To biologists, however, here was a hint that striped bass might be completing their entire life cycle in fresh water! This opened up a whole new field of happy speculation. Perhaps striped bass could thrive in fresh water! ·

1. This selection discusses the
   - □ a. enemies of the striped bass.
   - □ b. migration of the striped bass.
   - □ c. economic value of the striped bass.
   - □ d. family of the striped bass.

2. The striped bass
   - □ a. has been found in some inland lakes.
   - □ b. is a close relative of the shark.
   - □ c. raises its family in kelp beds.
   - □ d. cannot survive in freshwater.

3. Lake Marion and Lake Moultree were formed in
   - □ a. 1928.
   - □ b. 1930.
   - □ c. 1936.
   - □ d. 1941.

4. Which of the following seems to be true?
   - □ a. Striped bass are found in every state.
   - □ b. Lake Marion and Lake Moultree are man-made lakes.
   - □ c. Bass have always spawned in freshwater.
   - □ d. Young bass are not as healthy as their ancestors.

5. Another name for the striped bass is
   - □ a. dogfish.
   - □ b. rockfish.
   - □ c. parrot fish.
   - □ d. lion fish.

6. An angler is
   - □ a. a New Englander.
   - □ b. a scientist.
   - □ c. a fisherman.
   - □ d. an engineer.

CATEGORIES OF COMPREHENSION QUESTIONS

| No. 1: Subject Matter | No. 3: Supporting Details | No. 5: Clarifying Devices |
| No. 2: Main Idea | No. 4: Conclusion | No. 6: Vocabulary in Context |

25. NATURE'S FLYING MOUSETRAP

In spite of the beneficial service that birds of prey carry out for mankind, and in spite of laws to protect them, all too often any large bird flying across the countryside is likely to be on the receiving end of a load of birdshot. Why is this?

The usual excuse for this idiotic behavior goes something like this: "Well, I saw it flying around up there, and I just couldn't resist the opportunity." It seems an ironic twist of fate that birds of prey, such as hawks and eagles, have to suffer this senseless harassment while destructive rodents, which compete directly with man for food, go their merry way comparatively unmolested. Of course, rats and mice and other rodents don't go flying around the countryside. They do their dirty work at night or in grain storage bins where the damage is not noticed until too late.

Rodent damage costs farmers thousands of dollars every year, yet some farmers still persist in shooting at all hawks and birds of prey. In addition to breaking the law, they are literally robbing their own pockets by eliminating their natural allies.

Many misinformed hunters shoot at any large bird flying overhead under the mistaken impression that they are thereby helping game populations. The mistake here is that while birds of prey may occasionally take a game bird, it is not a major portion of their diet.

Like all other predators, birds of prey are opportunists. They take what comes easiest. The most abundant rodents in an area are also the easiest prey simply because they are numerous. Besides, if a hawk does happen to take a quail or pheasant once in a while, it usually is either crippled or sick. The healthy specimens escape rather easily and go on to improve the species. In fact, this is an excellent example of evolution working through natural selection: the weaker, less desirable individuals are eliminated; the strong, alert individuals survive.

With their keen eyes scanning the ground continuously, birds of prey are hunting their next meal. Any rat or mouse running across open ground or exposed to observation from above is fair game for these aerial exterminators.

Birds of prey, such as our hawks, are superbly equipped for their way of life. Probably the most efficient vision in the animal kingdom, together with sharp talons for grasping prey and strong, hooked beaks for tearing flesh, make birds of prey expert predators.

1. This passage is mainly about
   □ a. game birds.
   □ b. desert birds.
   □ c. song birds.
   □ d. birds of prey.

2. Choose the main idea of this article.
   □ a. Predatory birds are beneficial.
   □ b. Most rodents are helpful.
   □ c. Farmers protect their crops from rodents by pesticides.
   □ d. The game bird population is rapidly decreasing.

3. According to this selection, most rodents are
   □ a. opportunists.
   □ b. nocturnal.
   □ c. predators.
   □ d. fearsome.

4. We can guess that quail and pheasants are classified as
   □ a. game birds.
   □ b. song birds.
   □ c. predators.
   □ d. tropical birds.

5. Which of the following words best describes the rodents in this article?
   □ a. Useful
   □ b. Protective
   □ c. Destructive
   □ d. Quarrelsome

6. Aerial has to do with
   □ a. electricity.
   □ b. air.
   □ c. land.
   □ d. water.

CATEGORIES OF COMPREHENSION QUESTIONS

| No. 1: Subject Matter | No. 3: Supporting Details | No. 5: Clarifying Devices |
| No. 2: Main Idea | No. 4: Conclusion | No. 6: Vocabulary in Context |

ACKNOWLEDGEMENTS

The articles appearing in this booklet have been reprinted with the kind permission of the following publications and publishers to whom the author is indebted:

Aramco World Magazine, published by The Arabian American Oil Company, New York, New York.

The Communicator, published by the New York State Outdoor Education Association, Syracuse, New York.

The Conservationist, published by the New York State Conservation Department, Albany, New York.

A Cornell Science Leaflet, published by the New York State College of Agriculture and Life Sciences, a unit of the State University, at Cornell University, Ithaca, New York.

Food, The Yearbook of Agriculture, published by the United States Department of Agriculture, Washington, D.C.

Handbook of Nature-Study, published by Comstock Publishing Company, Ithaca, New York.

Kansas Fish & Game, published by the Kansas Forestry, Fish and Game Commission, Pratt, Kansas.

National Wildlife, published by The National Wildlife Federation, Washington, D.C.

Outdoor Oklahoma, published by the Oklahoma Department of Wildlife Conservation, Oklahoma City, Oklahoma.

Pennsylvania Game News, published by the Pennsylvania Game Commission, Harrisburg, Pennsylvania.

Ranger Rick's Nature Magazine, published by The National Wildlife Federation, Washington, D.C.

The Tennessee Conservationist, published by the Tennessee Department of Conservation and the Tennessee Game and Fish Commission.

ANSWER KEY

Passage 1:	1-b	2-d	3-c	4-a	5-a	6-d
Passage 2:	1-c	2-d	3-a	4-d	5-b	6-c
Passage 3:	1-b	2-a	3-d	4-c	5-a	6-d
Passage 4:	1-d	2-c	3-d	4-a	5-c	6-b
Passage 5:	1-b	2-d	3-a	4-d	5-c	6-c
Passage 6:	1-d	2-a	3-a	4-b	5-c	6-b
Passage 7:	1-d	2-c	3-d	4-a	5-b	6-d
Passage 8:	1-a	2-c	3-c	4-b	5-a	6-c
Passage 9:	1-b	2-a	3-d	4-a	5-b	6-d
Passage 10:	1-b	2-b	3-c	4-a	5-d	6-c
Passage 11:	1-b	2-c	3-c	4-d	5-c	6-d
Passage 12:	1-a	2-d	3-c	4-b	5-b	6-c
Passage 13:	1-a	2-c	3-a	4-b	5-a	6-d
Passage 14:	1-a	2-d	3-b	4-b	5-d	6-b
Passage 15:	1-b	2-b	3-b	4-a	5-c	6-b
Passage 16:	1-d	2-b	3-c	4-a	5-b	6-c
Passage 17:	1-c	2-a	3-c	4-a	5-b	6-d
Passage 18:	1-b	2-a	3-a	4-b	5-d	6-b
Passage 19:	1-d	2-a	3-b	4-d	5-b	6-c
Passage 20:	1-a	2-d	3-b	4-a	5-d	6-c
Passage 21:	1-b	2-d	3-b	4-c	5-c	6-d
Passage 22:	1-c	2-a	3-a	4-d	5-b	6-b
Passage 23:	1-c	2-b	3-d	4-a	5-b	6-c
Passage 24:	1-b	2-a	3-d	4-b	5-b	6-c
Passage 25:	1-d	2-a	3-b	4-a	5-c	6-b

DIAGNOSTIC CHART

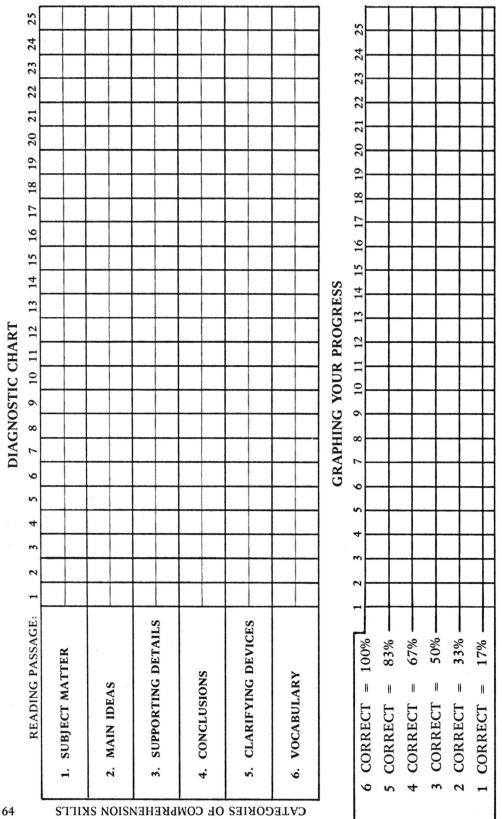

READING PASSAGE:	1	2	3	4	5	6	7	8	9	10	11	12	13	14	15	16	17	18	19	20	21	22	23	24	25
1. SUBJECT MATTER																									
2. MAIN IDEAS																									
3. SUPPORTING DETAILS																									
4. CONCLUSIONS																									
5. CLARIFYING DEVICES																									
6. VOCABULARY																									

CATEGORIES OF COMPREHENSION SKILLS

GRAPHING YOUR PROGRESS

	1	2	3	4	5	6	7	8	9	10	11	12	13	14	15	16	17	18	19	20	21	22	23	24	25
6 CORRECT = 100%																									
5 CORRECT = 83%																									
4 CORRECT = 67%																									
3 CORRECT = 50%																									
2 CORRECT = 33%																									
1 CORRECT = 17%																									

64